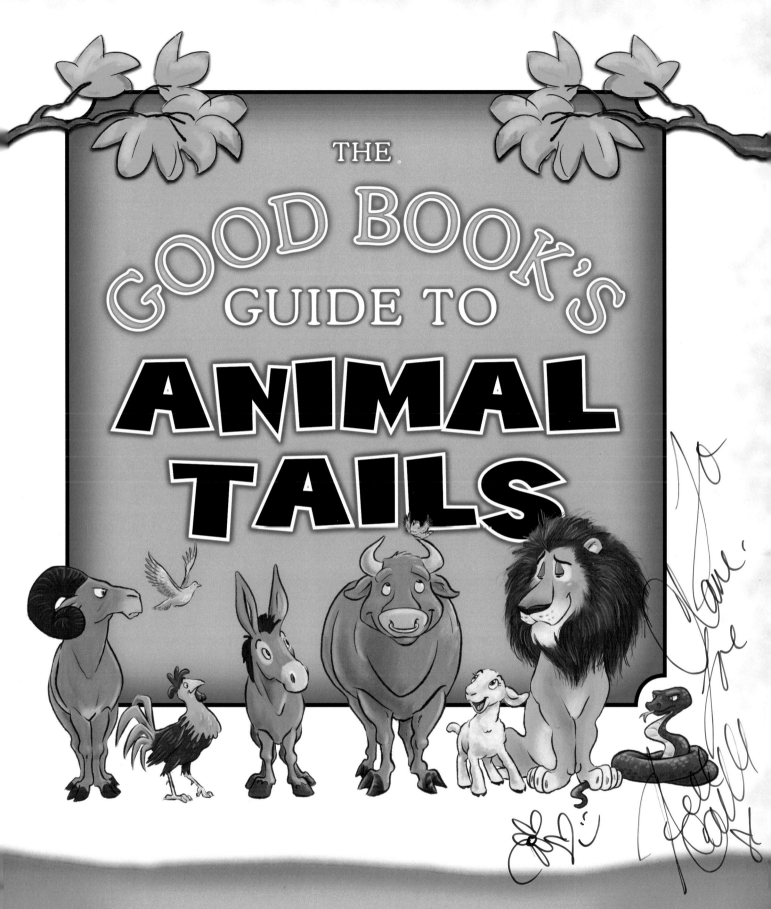

# THE
# GOOD BOOK'S
## GUIDE TO
# ANIMAL TAILS

## Nicole D. Cannella
### Illustrated by Tim Hodge

Lampion Press, LLC
P. O. Box 932
Silverton, OR 97381

ISBN: 978-1-942614-39-5

Library of Congress Control Number: 2018936337

Illustrations: Tim Hodge
Formatting and cover design: Amy Cole, JPL Design Solutions

Printed in the United States of America

# DEDICATION AND ACKNOWLEDGEMENTS

To my parents who paved my way, my friends, family and students who fanned the good flames and to my "rise tribe," thank you. To Dorian "DStrong Murray," my muse—you left a mark on my heart. To Jeff Kinney for furthering a fighter's wish for fame, and for creating a space in which I write and teach, thank you. To my illustrator who is an inspiration in faith and to Lampion Press, Tim Demy and Amy Cole for your vision. To Andy Stanley and North Point Church who were the conduit to my conversion, much gratitude. To my faithful children, Nick, Olivia and Noelle and my steadfastly supportive husband, Jerome, you have my heart. Most of all, to my Heavenly Father and True Vine. You are I AM. I know now I am the found coin.

It has been called many things—The Good Book, The Word, The original history text, and the Bible.

It is full of faith and triumphs; trials and redemption and...

# ANIMALS!

So many animals fill the Greatest Story ever told. From the Old Testament to the New Testament, animals weave through the tales of nobles and lowly; of kings, queens, and commoners.

The great storyteller C. S. Lewis stated he wished he had penned a book through the eyes of the biblical animals. This inspired us to do just that and to do it for children; to imagine what the world of the Bible and its people would have looked like through the eyes of the animals who were present.

From the ram beside Abraham to the donkey that carried Jesus, *Good Book's Guide to Animal Tails* brings the stories of the Bible to an endearing and unique new life.

See also the companion book for adults, *Creation Groans* written by Patrick Hunt.

# THE SERPENT

HOW SIMPLE IT WAS
TO DECEIVE THE GLAD GIRL—
TO WOO HER AWAY,
FROM HER WHOLE, KNOWN, SAFE WORLD.

I did not come
in snake-like form,
I did not approach her
all battered and torn.

I came as enticing—
as beauty itself,
and lured Eve away
with cunning and stealth.

My smooth and slippery
whispers of deceit,
brought all of their focus—
to that one forbidden tree.

One tree that God warned them
to avoid at all costs—
one tree that would lead them
from found to so lost.

God desired that He
have Heaven and Earth too—
but I had a plan
for Him and for you…

…A plan to pull all away
just like I did Adam and Eve—
to steal and destroy
like a slippery thief.

My ways of distracting them
from all of God's grace—
I use on all people,
I lie to each face.

I'm called the "prince of this earth"
by Jesus, Himself—
I will rob you of joy,
of faith, and good health.

Sure, I now slither
as I slink on the ground—
eat dust and get stepped on
by He with the crown…

But it's worth it if I
can lure His loved ones away—
just like I did Eve and Adam
that fateful day.

I deter all from seeing
the good all around—
as I look up at them
from this dusty, cold ground.

There are rumors this will end
with His foot on my head—
but until then my plan is
to fill His people with dread.

So listen here,
and heed only my advice—
as I skulk on rock bottom
eating dust, dirt, and mice.

Don't listen to His words
or that still, small voice from above—
because wouldn't you rather feel anger
than love?

Learn more about
the tricky snake:
GENESIS 3:1-7

5

# ABEL'S SHEEP

**I** AM A SHEEP
FROM ANTIQUITY—
FROM OLD TESTAMENT CAME I
BEFORE AS BABY, CAME HE.

Although Jesus was there
in Trinity form—
far back in Genesis time,
before I was born.

You see, I belonged
to a young man named Abel—
I followed him daily,
between farmlands and stable.

I lifted my eyes
to witness each day—
two brothers:
one grounded, one going astray.

I had heard of a serpent
who led Adam and Eve,
from their perfect homeland—
called the Garden of Eden.

I learned how his trickery
had led them away—
as a sheep I understood
their temptation that day.

The temptation to roam;
to go off on your own—
and the need for a Shepherd
to guide us all home.

We fragile, lost creatures
so desperate for Shepherd,
need guidance and steering—
for our gentle tempers…

…can lead us astray,
to tread down wrong paths—
so we seek a strong leader
with rod and with staff.

I am a sheep,
from the Genesis story
a witness to two sons—
one who basked in God's glory,

The other held back
the best of his crop—
feeling he was deserving
of the fresh share on top.

And though he loved me
with all of his heart
dear Abel, he knew—
I was one set apart—

Born with no markings—
no bruise nor dark spot in sight,
he would sacrifice me
and I would put up no fight.

I was thankful and seeking
to get back to sweet Heaven—
for like Eden before me—
it is a place without blemish.

And as Abel gave me
to our Creator that night—
God looked down from His throne
on Abel with delight.

But God was upset
with cantankerous Cain—
who believed God did nothing
for the profits He gained.

God sent Cain a message
that he'd failed a divine test—
He knew Cain was self righteous,
and should have given his best.

Well, Cain got so angry
with God's reprimand—
that he hurt his dear brother
with his very own hands.

And our God heard a crying;
a sad, prayerful call…
then He wept for his sons—
who had suffered the fall.

The good news is Abel
and I are together—
with our Maker,
where we bask in God's
    blessing forever.

And what came of Cain?
You may start to wonder…
he was punished with consequence
of having to wander…

…To wander this planet—
never feeling quite full,
still, his God was beside him—
and he'd feel His pull…

…A pull toward Heaven—
where he sent Abel that day
where two brothers can reconcile
and cast anger away.

I'm just a small sheep—
unblemished, it's true.
and I am so blessed to share
this Bible story with you.

Meet Abel and
his lamb here:
GENESIS 4:4,
HEBREWS 11:4

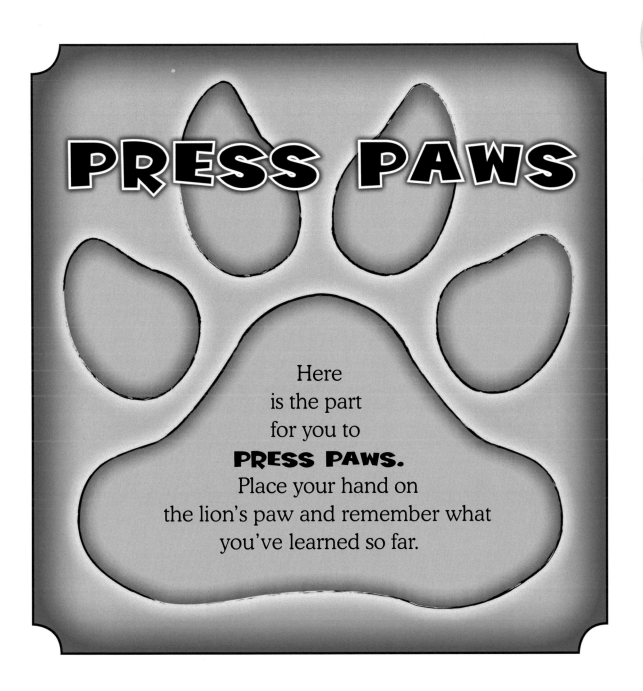

# PRESS PAWS

Here
is the part
for you to
**PRESS PAWS.**
Place your hand on
the lion's paw and remember what
you've learned so far.

The serpent tricked Adam and Eve
to disobey their God above—
and even though He was upset,
God still covered them with love.

Abel was faithful to the Father—
and gave to Him his favorite lamb,
now turn the page to read about
the ram who helped Abraham!

# ISAAC'S RAM

I STOOD BEHIND THE THICKET OF SHRUBBERY AND VINES— WAITING TO HEAR THE WONDROUS WORD SENT FROM GOD DIVINE.

Abraham was his full name
and he was God's elect
to be a father of our faith—
an honor he'd accept.

Abraham was told by God
to lead His chosen nation—
the followers of His great name;
a speaker for creation.

Abraham took a leap of faith
and so the angels said,
"You will have a son to raise—
Since you accepted to be led."

Sarah, his wife, she laughed at this
and thought it was a joke—
but anything was possible
when the God of Heaven spoke.

"Name him Isaac," they were told
because of Sarah's laughter—
Isaac means "to laugh aloud"
he'll be known for ever after.

Abe and Sarah were not young
so she was quick to doubt,
but when Isaac was born at last—
there was much to smile about.

Isaac was a loving son—
and Abe was always with him,
then one day, Abe heard God's word—
and knew that he must listen.

God told faithful Abraham
to take Isaac up the hill
and give him to our mighty Lord—
(God had to test Abe's will.)

Abe did as God had wanted
because he knew inside,
the Lord would spare their sacred son
he was certain He'd provide—

And so Abe said, "We will be back."
As he climbed that hill, so tall—
Isaac asked, "Where is the ram
that we shall give to God?"

Abe did not know two crucial things
as he climbed intensely praying—
one was that God would give His Son—
and the other, that I was waiting,

When they reached the very top
and Abe prepared goodbyes—
I stepped out from the shrubbery
and let out a loud cry.

I did not cry for fear or worry—
it was a bleat of joy.
For I knew God had prepared me
to step in for that young boy.

So I got to go in Isaac's place—
to Heaven, perfect and sweet—
While Abraham and his dear son,
made Bible history.

Get to know Isaac's ram:
**GENESIS 22:13**

Lions once were plant eaters,
not always primal beasts—
Eden was filled with fruits and herbs—
of which we were blessed to feast.

Then came the fall and creation
    groaned—
later my pride and I
recalled a time in Eden land—
when beasts let out a cry.

We were not made to long—
for meals of meat and bone…
God designed us to dine on that—
which grew from ground alone.

But since the day the liar's whisper—
crept into young Eve's ear,
we are now the king of predators—
a breed that evokes fear.

He called us "lion," the Adam man—
a breed majestic and so grand,
once we roamed in peace with
    the meek—
we lions laid with lambs.

Now, however, we are born
to crave and hunt and desire—
meals of meat and tender bone,
since Eden's fall transpired.

Now I, and my pride were captured—
and made to live in a den
where sad, poor souls were tossed
    inside
to meet their bitter end.

Our job was clear, make them
    our meal
and this, we must oblige…
it did not matter young or old—
big or small in size.

And then one night a man named Dan,
or Daniel, if you will—
was dropped into our darkened den—
expectant we would kill.

We moved on instinct that fateful eve,
poised and set to pounce—
but God stopped our paws right in
    their tracks,
we weren't to eat one once.

The Spirit of God, our great Creator—
gently shut our lips—
with hands as soft as sifting sand—
He commanded us to sit.

And sit we did until sleep came—
Daniel resting on our heads—
with calm deep breaths on warmth
    of fur
Dan went from feast to friend!

Say hello to Daniel's lion:
**DANIEL 6:22**

13

# JONAH'S WHALE

**J**ONAH WAS A PROPHET—
THAT'S A FANCY WAY TO SAY,
HE COULD TELL THE FUTURE
WHILE USING GOD'S GREAT NAME.

Jonah had been very brave
up until the day—
he was told to go to Nineveh,
but he ran the other way.

Well not exactly "ran;" you see—
a ship is what he rode—
to try to flee God's plan for him—
to escape what he was told…

…told to do by God, Himself—
he was meant to go and tell
the people of old Nineveh,
they were not behaving well.

Nineveh was a nasty place
a crime filled neighborhood—
and Jonah did not see how they
could ever be of good.

Headed far from Nineveh—
was a ship he jumped aboard
in his mind he told himself
he'd be safe on other shores…

…ones opposite of Nineveh
where he could hide from God
"Maybe He'll forget His plan—
perhaps He already forgot?"

Well God does not forget, you see—
and Jonah learned that quick
for beneath the ship that very night
the tide was turning quick…

(…and they all were feeling sick!)

The waves grew huge; far too intense
and it distressed the crew—
they shouted out among themselves
"Oh no, what do we do?"

"Throw me over!" Jonah yelled
above the winds' loud cry
"I'm the one who upset my God
I'm the guilty guy."

"We can't just toss him over!"
The crewman said in shock —
but Jonah became brave and said
"What other choice ya got?"

Toss him in the sea, they did—
with it's mighty waves that rolled
and I opened up my massive mouth
and swallowed the prophet whole.

I was careful not to hurt the guy—
not one part of him was marked
I had one job to do that night,
I swallowed him in the dark.

I was to give him the chance to see
our God is above all—
His plan was to set Nineveh free
and Jonah ignored His call.

Three days sat he there in my belly
among the fish, and muck, and sea—
until he realized God needed him
to be the prophet he could be.

There in my hollow stomach—
I heard Jonah cry aloud
"I'm sorry Lord, for you were there…
you didn't let me drown!

I see that's what you want
for all your children.
Your plan is to give grace to all—
so I will go and tell them."

And when Heaven let me know
that Jonah had repented
I opened my jaws and spit him out
and to Nineveh He sent him.

Jonah shared Heaven's grace
with all those Ninevites
and when they had accepted God—
Jonah still thought twice.

He wondered how the worst of us
could ever be forgiven
he cried under hot desert skies
and a vine grew there to shade him.

But a worm came through and chewed
up that sweet and shady vine
Jonah melted down again
crying "Why God, why ?"

God scolded His son Jonah
for not seeing the big scene
the good and bad deserve God's
    grace—
we forgive our enemies.

Jonah never understood
the bigness of God's vision—
so when God calls you to do a job
even if it's scary…

Just listen.

Imagine swimming with
Jonah's whale, here:
**JONAH 1:17**

# PRESS PAWS

Time to touch
the lion's paw and
recall what you have
learned so far!

Abraham and Isaac were so
   relieved to see—
A ram burst through the
   thorny vines
and make Bible history.

The lions did not bite or harm
Daniel in that den—

They closed their mouths and
   obeyed God,
to become Daniel's friends.

Jonah did not listen to
What God had to say—
He was tested out in the deep sea,
when he tried to run away.

# NATIVITY OX

LOOKED AND SAW THE SHINING STAR,
THE ONE I'D HEARD THEM SPEAK OF—
MANY PEOPLE HAD PREDICTED
IT WOULD BE THE ONE TO LEAD THEM...

...lead them to the One true King
that we oxen, cows and lambs
knew from the beginning
when created by His hand.

And when we heard He'd come to earth
as a little babe—
we too were eager to see the boy
that lay within the stable.

I watched as the nervous Joseph man
led tired Mary inside—
to prepare for her a small, safe place
under starry skies.

She did not have a warm, soft bed
and neither did the babe—
they both were made to lay upon
scattered cloths and hay.

When He was born the King of kings
we oxen all did bow—
we knew Him in the Eden land
and we all still know Him now.

My oxen heart, it skipped a beat
as the Son of God cried out—
then as he lay there peacefully
there was not any doubt…

Our great Father had come to earth
in tiny baby form—
to lead His sons and daughters
in the Way, the Truth, the Word.

I witnessed as the shepherd men,
came to pay respects—
and three wise kings from the
        Far East—
they all did genuflect.

Which means they each fell to
        their knees
and I am still so grateful—
to have been a part of history
that night there in the stable.

Imagine meeting the
Ox from the stable here:
LUKE 2:7

MARY AND JOSEPH GOT THE WORD THAT THEY WOULD HAVE TO TRAVEL— AND GO TO HAVE THEIR JESUS BLESSED BY PRIESTS INSIDE THE TEMPLE.

They walked a long, long way
and when the three arrived—
they were met by an old man,
who fell to his knees and cried.

He was so thankful to see Jesus
held by his mother, Mary—
he reached out slender, shaking hands
while his wrinkled eyes grew teary.

"I knew that I would see the day
that I would hold my Lord—
God showed me in a dream, you see
and told me in His Word…

…that before I passed to Heaven—
I'd meet the One True King,
you cannot know the years I've longed
or the joy that you three bring"

I watched as they spoke on that
        dusty road—
and heard what the old man said
I saw as he held Jesus tight
and kissed his sweet, soft head.

We had travelled with Mary and Joseph
to be given up to Heaven—
for when they met the Temple priests
a gift was to be given.

I was not afraid at all
and neither was my twin
to be given as an offering—
(we would do it all again).

For I was there that day to see
that waiting old man weep—
I felt such peace inside my heart,
that I fell straight to sleep.

And when I woke up with my twin
together we did meet—
our very own Creator
and sat there by His feet.

We knew what we'd been born for—
and why we were called Home.
We flew high above with angels,
around Heaven's holy throne.

God knew what would happen
with me, Mary and that man—
every moment God prepared
as part of His great plan.

I am a white and wondrous dove
as is my little twin—
and we were part of a Bible tale
that you can now share in!

Imagine the pure white
feathers of Mary's doves
here: LUKE 2:24

# JESUS' DONKEY

I AM A MERE DONKEY,
SOME SEE JUST A SMALL HORSE—
BUT I CARRIED OUR LORD ONE FATEFUL DAY
AS HE CHARTERED HIS HOLY COURSE.

His course and his path—
so dusty and harsh,
to die on a cross—
and win back your hearts.

He knew I'd be there—
so His disciples, He tested,
in faith—soon to see
I'd be waiting… predestined.

He told his good friends
to go locate my owner,
so they could untether me
and free me go.

And as Jesus sat
on my small, bony back
I carried Him proudly—
though large presence I lacked.

As crowds of thousands
chanted loud and laid palms—
we trotted so slowly,
my dear Lord remained calm.

Though He was aware—
that they who laid palms
would all soon betray Him,
for He caused them alarm.

Those who had chanted—
so loudly that day—
would accept Him no longer…
would give Him away.

I watched from afar
that sad afternoon—
as our Savior—
He suffered, lonely in gloom.

How I wished I could carry Him
straight back from that town—
to a place of sweet safety,
with no cross and no crown.

But alas, He did know
as He sat on my spine,
how it all would unfold—
how the stars would align.

The day was as gray
as my very own fur—
and I bowed my head low
as He suffered and hurt.

Jesus forged through somehow—
despite pain, despite fear—
so one day our God
could wipe away all our tears.

And before He breathed last
He offered prayer pure and true—
"Forgive them, my Father…
for they know not what they do."

I'm just a mere donkey—
a gray speckle of creation,
but I carried The One
who saves you and all nations!

See more about
Jesus' donkey:
**MATTHEW 21:2**

23

# PETER'S ROOSTER

**J**ESUS TOLD PETER THAT IT WOULD BE SO
HE SAID, "BEFORE THE ROOSTER CROWS—
3 TIMES YOU'LL SAY YOU DID NOT KNOW...
YOU'LL SAY YOU DID NOT KNOW ME.

I am that rooster that He spoke of
the one Jesus foretold—
I am the Rooster who crowed
    three times—
that morning in the cold.

Now, Peter—he was called "The Rock,"
a nickname Jesus gave—
He said that Peter was so strong,
he needed a new name.

Rocks are solid and sturdy—
they don't freeze nor do they puddle,
as Peter did that fateful day—
that Jesus was in trouble.

Before that, at a supper—
I heard Dear Jesus say;
"One of you will tell on me,
and one will turn away."

Peter became so upset,
he cried, "Not me, not I…
I would never turn from You—
I would rather die."

"But Peter," Jesus said that night,
"I'm afraid that it is true—
three times you will be asked
if I was friend to you.

You will reply to each of them,
'I do not know that man.'
And when they all pull me away—
from afar you'll stand."

He may have walked on water
with Jesus one sweet day—
but when he feared he may die too—
Peter went astray.

When Christ came back from in that tomb
He sought Peter on a beach—
He said to his friend, "Hello again…
come, have breakfast with me."

He asked him there on that sand—
"Peter, do you love me true?"
and three times Peter answered Him,
"My Lord, You know I do."

Jesus smiled and touched his hand—
He told him, "Feed my sheep."
(Which meant He wanted Peter to go
and preach for you and me).

I did not want to crow that day;
I longed to grant a favor—
I hoped so much that Pete would say,
"I know Him, He's our Savior."

I see now a greater plan—
for Peter could have perished too—
if he had said the day Christ died,
"I'll die along with You."

Jesus had a plan for Peter;
a mission for His friend,
His Rock was meant to spread
    God's word…
so we all could understand.

Visit Peter's Rooster
here: MARK 14:72

# JESUS' SPARROW

I AM A LITTLE SPARROW
WHO SAT UPON CHRIST'S HAND—
I HAD NO FEAR OF MY CREATOR,
THE WAY I DID WITH MAN.

I was skittish around the sons
     of man—
around the daughters too,
but when God used me in His plan
I knew just what to do.

A parable is a lesson told
in a story way—
a means for friends to understand
what one is trying to say.

He used me as an example
to teach a parable—
He told His friends to, "Have no fear—
of something terrible…

For terror cannot ruin you
nor can anyone,
now that you've come to follow me—
God's one true Holy Son."

The disciples stared with widened eyes
and tried to understand,
as Jesus declared their destiny—
He held me in His hand.

I then flew high above their heads
to show His good example—
Tis true we birds don't want for much
we know that we are cared for.

Jesus said that faith filled day—
"Consider you, the sparrows,
they eat and nest and fly and play—
with no worry of tomorrow.

I wish to teach you, my beloveds—
to try and be like birds,
to seek and reach your destinies—
without fear of being hurt.

For no matter what befalls you
I am by your side—
and will be in each one of you,
until we meet on high.

I may know the very count
of feathers on birds of flight,
but I treasure each hair upon
     your heads
and I will guide you day and night."

He tells you not to worry—
He told them that day too,
He said if God protects the birds…
how much more He'll care for you.

I'm just a little sparrow—
small and black and white
but I was there the day God taught
to keep us sparrows in your sight!

Fly with Jesus' little
sparrows here:
MATTHEW 10:29

27

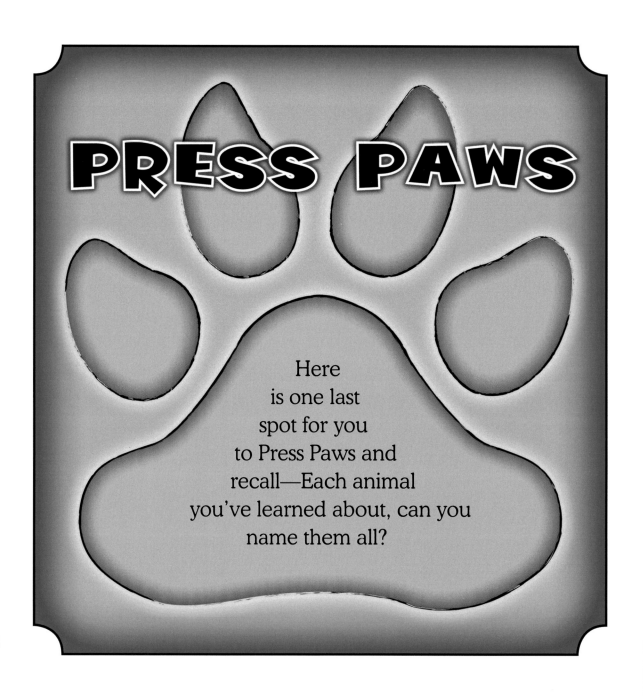

# PRESS PAWS

Here
is one last
spot for you
to Press Paws and
recall—Each animal
you've learned about, can you
name them all?

How did each animal help God's plan?
Who is your favorite one?
See if you can name them all—
when this *Good Book's Guide* is done.

God had a plan for each of them and He has a plan for you!